Improve Your Social Skills

Learn how to talk to people:

improve your charisma, increase your self-esteem and overcome your fears. Discover how to make friends and build healthy relationships

© **Copyright 2019 - All rights reserved.**

The content contained within this book may not be reproduced, duplicated or transmitted without direct written permission from the author or the publisher.

Under no circumstances will any blame or legal responsibility be held against the publisher, or author, for any damages, reparation, or monetary loss due to the information contained within this book, either directly or indirectly.

Legal Notice:
This book is copyright protected. It is only for personal use. You cannot amend, distribute, sell, use, quote or paraphrase any part, or the content within this book, without the consent of the author or publisher.

Disclaimer Notice:
Please note the information contained within this document is for educational and entertainment purposes only. All effort has been executed to present accurate, up to date, reliable, complete information. No warranties of any kind are declared or implied. Readers acknowledge that the author is not engaging in the rendering of legal, financial, medical or professional advice. The content within this book has been derived from various sources. Please consult a licensed professional before attempting any techniques outlined in this book.

By reading this document, the reader agrees that under no circumstances is the author responsible for any losses, direct or indirect, that are incurred as a result of the use of information contained within this document, including, but not limited to, errors, omissions, or inaccuracies.

Table of Contents

Introduction 1
Chapter 1: What Are Social Skills? 5
   Identify Your Strengths and Weaknesses 13
      Observing Patterns 14
      Trying New Hobbies 17
Chapter 2: Listening Skills 21
   Passive vs. Active 23
      Passive 23
      Active 25
   Empathy and Understanding 28
Chapter 3: Conversation Skills 35
   Combat Shyness 36
   Boost Your Charisma and Self-Esteem 40
   Overcome Your Fears and Insecurities 44
Chapter 4: Why is Socializing So Difficult? 49
   How to Challenge Your Inner Critic 51
   Acknowledging Disappointment and Failure 56
   Understanding the Difference Between Assertive and Aggressive 60
Chapter 5: Good Manners 65
   Why They Are Important 69
   Ways That Manners Are Forgotten 73
Chapter 6: Body Language 79
   Practical Application 85
Chapter 7: How to Meet New People 91
   Confidence 93
   Talking to Strangers 96
   Talking with Peers 98
   Building Connections 101
Chapter 8: Deepening Your Current Friendships 105
   How to Be You 112
Conclusion 115
Bibliography 119

5

Introduction

Excellent social skills allow you to present your best self to those around you. They can provide you with the confidence to succeed in all situations, and the ability to get to know the people you would like to become close to. From being able to identify your strengths to knowing exactly how to carry on a conversation, your social skills will provide you with deeper social connections. No matter who you are talking to, it is a considerable boost in confidence to be able to converse, socialize, and generally get to know another person. This connectivity is what makes you feel secure in yourself and your interactions.

While socialization is profound and essential, it can be difficult for some. Working up the courage to talk to another person can often be intimidating, especially when you are unsure of yourself. Many people struggle with their social skills, wishing that they were better at the skills that come naturally to some. With practice, the techniques in this guide are meant to build you up so that you feel comfortable and confident about socializing, no matter where you are or where you go. From working on your body language to discovering how to talk to new people, you will obtain a renewed sense of confidence in yourself.

Starting at the very beginning, you will learn about the skills that you already possess. By harnessing your strengths, your weaknesses will be easier to overcome. Instead of feeling ashamed that you have weaknesses, you will learn how to transform them into traits that will make socialization easier. If shyness is a burden in your life, you will learn how to combat it in ways that still allow you to feel comfortable while also appearing more extroverted. With a simple boost to your charisma from growing your self-esteem, you will feel capable enough to handle any social interaction that comes your way.

One of the hardest parts about socialization comes when you interact with new people. Because they are new to your life, you usually do not have any sense of comfort or familiarity to rely on. By learning how to confidently begin conversations and find commonalities with others, you will see that building connections with new people is possible. No matter how difficult it feels in the beginning, socialization is always something that becomes easier the more you do it.

The current relationships that you hold in your life are essential, too. Once you have become acquainted with someone, you must make sure that you maintain this connection by putting in the effort to socialize with them. This guide will teach you how to do this by providing you with tips and tricks that you can utilize in various social settings. By the time you have adopted these new habits, you will be able to talk to anyone, anywhere; and you will no longer be hindered by your doubts or worries about socialization. The skills that you gain will stay with you for life, a permanent reminder that it is possible for you to socialize successfully.

Chapter 1: What Are Social Skills?

Social skills are verbal and physical traits that we all possess. Some people thrive on social interaction, feeling energized after conversing with people. Others find the action intimidating, feeling nervous or anxious about the idea of having to interact with another person. No matter what your stance on social interaction is or what skills you currently have, there is no need to compare yourself to others. You are a unique individual with your own set of social skills and your own preferences. Whether you are introverted or extroverted, the skills that you have are part of who you are as a person.

Naturally, human beings are social creatures. We crave social interaction, even if it makes us nervous sometimes, which is quite normal. The idea is daunting to some because there is no standard of how you must think, act or behave. While there are social norms, morals, and taboos, you cannot guarantee that yours will match someone else's. This is why it is important to get to know someone, to learn and understand the deeper layers that make up their personality and find out what they believe in.

Think about the things that you are truly passionate about. It is probably easier for you to have a discussion about something you are passionate about than something you aren't as familiar with. Finding commonality is important when it comes to socialization as it allows you to have better social skills simply because you know what to say to the other person. We often take on interactions that challenge us and try to conform to what we believe others want us to be. It is important to change that mentality. As you interact with people in the future, work on presenting your true authentic self to them.

Consider your influences. You have developed into the person that you are today based on your likes, dislikes, and the things that inspire you. The people who you have spent the most time around have the biggest impact on your social skills. When people spend a lot of time together, they tend to pick up on one another's habits. Understand that everyone else you interact with has also been influenced by these same factors throughout their lives. While you might have grown up with the knowledge that using proper manners is the only way to show respect, someone else might have grown up being taught something entirely different.

If you can accept these differences before you begin with any social interaction, you might feel less of a need to change any part of yourself. Being worried about how someone else's perception of you isn't going to change the behavioral traits and personality that you already possess. It is far easier to just be yourself from the very beginning and let others respond to it. You do not need to 'explain' yourself or feel guilty about being different than the people around you. Celebrate these differences when you can. Know that they make you unique and interesting, and those other people should feel excited to talk to you because of your unique traits and quirks.

With socialization comes a fair share of rejection and disappointment. You might clash with someone because of their personality or you might have opposing views on the world. Other times, you just won't get along for no deeper reason. Learn how to accept this and move forward. You do not need to make sure that everyone likes and accepts you in order to be a whole person. You are whole on your own, and you should only want to socialize with those who feel the same way about you. People have the ability to disappoint you because of expectations. Because of your standards, you might be expecting a certain level of behavior, only to find out that other people do not value it the same way that you do. In these instances, it is also important to reach a point of acceptance and keep moving forward.

Being resentful of the differences you discover in other people will only make you feel alienated. This is what causes social anxiety. Do your best to let go of these things because it becomes a burden to hold onto them. When you are able to accept that certain people are just not meant to be a part of your life, it becomes easier to have conversations with them. Taking risks is the only way that you will find out for sure. This is one of the most fun parts about socialization, too; you never know what the interaction might develop into.

The following are some examples of what you would consider social skills:

- Good Manners: When you have good manners, you are presenting yourself as a kind and respectful person. This is important if you'd like to show people that you are open for social interactions. If you have ever wanted to start a conversation with someone, yet they were displaying bad manners, it is likely that you did not follow through. Keep in mind that showcasing your good manners will benefit you socially. You will be able to show people that you are capable of being nice and being socially interactive.

- Cooperation: Some situations aren't going to benefit you. For example, if you want to eat at a certain restaurant but your friends all want to eat elsewhere, you would come to a compromise if you agreed to eat at the place that they preferred. This is a courtesy done out of having good social etiquette. Being an agreeable person will make your life a lot easier than protesting every little thing that you disagree with. It is important that you carefully weigh your options, determining if the opposition is worth it.

- Praising Others: When you notice that someone is doing well, a simple expression of praise can be a kind gesture. This is a great social skill to have because it is one that is based on kindness. When you give praise, make sure that you are expressing it honestly. Anything that is forced or dishonest will hinder your relationship with this person because you aren't being genuine. It is better to say nothing than to lie about praise that you do not truly want to give.

- Positive Communication: No one wants to speak with someone, only to find out that they will be discussing negative things. When you communicate with others, try to keep the negativity to a minimum if you can help it.

Naturally, you will have some serious conversations in your life, but they do not all have to revolve around negativity. The way you present your dialogue will heavily impact how people will perceive it. By using a kind tone and having a pleasant attitude, you can ensure that people do not confuse the message that you are trying to convey.

- Accepting Differences: Much like you must accept the many quirks and eccentricities in yourself, you must also accept the differences of others. Not everyone will think exactly like you or believe in what you believe in, and that is okay. Tolerance is essential for maintaining great social skills. While you do not have to change your entire outlook, you also don't need to bash other people for what they believe in. Having the ability to accept differences will allow you to talk to people who are different from you without creating controversy.

- Active Listening: There is a difference between hearing what you would like to hear and actually listening to what a person is trying to express. Your listening skills make up a big part of your social skills. The ability to listen to what someone is trying to say before you come up with a response is important. It shows that you care about what the other person is saying while also enforcing the point that you are paying attention. Many people who struggle socially find that conversing is difficult because they are too quick to jump in with a response. Practice active listening. Let the other person communicate their thoughts in entirety before you reply or ask questions. Recap some of their thoughts or statements as a way to show them you're actively listening and that you genuinely want to understand them and how you can help them or be there for them. This will help you better develop a conversation.

- Helping Others: When you approach a person with the intention that you would like to help them, you are displaying a set of social skills that comes from a very caring place. While it is still a good idea to verify if the opposite person would like your help before you begin helping them, it can be a way for you to bond and express your nurturing side. A lot of the time, using this nurturing ability is a great way to further develop your social skills. It feels great to be kind, and the other person will feel just as great knowing that you care enough to help.

- Being Respectful: Having a level of respect for yourself and others is a way for you to maintain a likable personality. When you are respectful, people will not be deterred from talking to you or interacting with you. It can be off-putting when a person seems interesting, yet they are disrespectful. For a lot of people, this can be an immediate deal-breaker. Just as you wouldn't want to interact with someone who is disrespectful, it is important to make sure that you are not portraying yourself in this way either.

- Resolving Conflicts: Arguments are draining and time-consuming. When you have the ability to resolve conflicts, you are more likely to have successful interactions with others. When conflicts only seem to continue and get worse by the minute, it is likely that those involved have no intention of resolving it. These are people who enjoy the tension and the challenge. It is a lot easier to simply reach a singular conclusion by working with the person and establishing common ground than opposing them and trying to dominate the argument.

Identify Your Strengths and Weaknesses

We all have them, the traits that make up what we are good at and what we fall short on. Identifying these parts of yourself will allow you to better understand what your strengths are. When you know your strengths, you can utilize them to your advantage during social interactions. Being able to fall back on your strengths can be very comforting, especially if socialization makes you nervous. Your weaknesses can also be transformed to serve you during social situations. Instead of letting them hold you back, you can learn how to work with them and apply them in positive ways.

Make a list of all the things that you are good at. Do not spend too much time focusing on each thing. Simply write down the first things that come to mind. Next, write down the things that you wish you were better at. Seeing both on paper is a way for you to assess who you are as a person. These are the traits that allow you to act the way that you do and think the way that you do. Don't be hard on yourself as you work on your list. There is no need to feel shame or guilt because we all have things that we could work on about ourselves.

You are taking the first step toward self-growth when you identify the things that you would like to change or improve about yourself. Being able to see everything that you desire gives you the motivation to apply real changes to your life to accomplish these things. Accept your weaknesses and think about ways in which you can turn them into strengths. You might be nervous about speaking to people in a group setting, but you excel in having one-on-one conversations. Work on this by slowly increasing the number of people that you speak to at once. Discuss a topic that you are passionate about. Before you know it, you will be able to express yourself in front of a room full of people.

Know that you do not have to make these changes all at once. Getting stronger is a process that involves many steps. You might have to repeat certain steps before you truly take them on as new habits. Repeat them as many times as you need to feel confident in who you are. Make goals for yourself that will push you to do better without stressing you out. Practice your newfound strengths by expressing them to people that you are close to. The familiarity will allow you to focus on yourself rather than what the other person thinks of you.

Observing Patterns

On your quest to identify what you are good at and what you need to work on, pay attention to any patterns or triggers that occur. You can learn a lot about your behaviors and traits by observing your surroundings. Think about the things that you value most. They will be the guiding factors that shape your behaviors. For example, if you get nervous around large groups of people, this will likely trigger shyness or a reserved attitude. It is important that you learn how to simply observe without being too hard on yourself. You do not need to rush to change anything about yourself. This exercise is only meant for you to learn more about yourself.

As you pick up on these situations that trigger you, acknowledge that your response is entirely normal. Everyone holds a different personality, so their reactions and responses will vary. What is thrilling to someone might be anxiety-inducing to you. The trick is to fully accept who you are as a person. Maybe you are shy or maybe you enjoy talking to others but have difficulty keeping the conversation flowing. No matter what the case is, there is always room for improvement. Not only does improving your social skills benefit your ability to talk to other people, but it also builds up the confidence that you have in yourself.

Once you have reached a point of acceptance, the next step is to push yourself a little bit. Go outside your comfort zone. This does not mean that you need to put yourself in situations where you feel completely uncomfortable, but you should aim for trying new things every once in a while. For example, if you feel awkward or uncomfortable being around large groups of people, try to hang out with your friends in a group setting. While it is only temporary, you will have the comfort and familiarity of your friends while also being around other people. Actions like these make it possible for you to get used to the idea of being within a group setting.

Make a promise to yourself that you will work on facing your social fears slowly but surely. As long as you can commit to trying out new situations, then you will be able to move past your existing fears. Speak to those who are closest to you about some of the fears that you have. They might be willing to guide you through them and help you work on your social anxiety if you have any. It helps to have familiarity around you because it works as a form of encouragement. Instead of pushing yourself to socialize with complete strangers in a large group, you will be taking the action steps which is exactly what you should be doing.

The idea is to let go of the mentality that the very worst thing is going to happen to you. Fears have a way of taking over us, and they will severely impact you if you let them. A common social fear is doing or saying something embarrassing within a group of people. This can be debilitating to some, and it can even prevent them from entering any social situations altogether. Instead of focusing on this one potential outcome, do your best to enter every social situation with an open mind. Consider that nobody is out there for the sole purpose of judging you. Chances are, they are worried about their own behavior and how you are going to perceive them. No matter how confident a person is, there is always a chance that they care what you think of them too.

Trying New Hobbies

Picking up some new skills might allow you to feel better about your current skills. There are several things that you can try for the purpose of broadening your strengths. From crafting to salsa dancing, pick an activity that you have always wanted to try but haven't started yet. Remember that you will be a beginner, so try not to judge yourself as you try out these new hobbies. The only thing that you should be focusing on is your enjoyment level. Do you like this? Is this not for you? The great part is, this is solely up to you to decide. If you end up trying something but not liking it, you can stop and move onto the next hobby. The freedom to choose is all yours which is a great feeling.

If you end up picking something you like, that is great! Continue doing it as long as it makes you happy. Thinking about things from a bigger perspective, such as potentially getting involved with a new social circle because of your newfound interest. There are so many ways that taking on a new hobby can not only benefit the strengths that you already have but also the ways in which you meet new people. When you push yourself in this way, you are promoting growth. The following are some examples of how certain hobbies can allow you to grow and experience new possibilities:

- Creative Hobbies: Painting, drawing, dancing, writing, and singing are all excellent things for you to try. They are fun, and they allow you to express yourself in a different way, aside from speaking. The best part is, you can utilize tutorial videos online to teach yourself how to do these things or you can opt for taking classes or lessons. The versatility and flexibility make creative hobbies seem attainable.

Once you find something that you really like, you can seek out other people who are also interested in these activities. Becoming a part of a dance class, for example, can broaden your social circle in a way that wasn't possible before you took up the hobby. From the very beginning, you will have something in common with the rest of the group which gives you automatic topics of conversation.

It can also help to become a part of a group because you will be able to talk through your problems or doubts with people who are going through the same experiences. This feeling of togetherness can be enough to soothe your worries about fitting in or doing the right thing. You might even be able to find additional encouragement which will motivate you to become better yourself. As soon as you open one door, it is likely that several more possibilities will become available to you. The hardest part is just taking the first step.

- Practical Hobbies: An example of a practical hobby is something that is fun but also useful in your daily life. Taking up cooking can serve this purpose. As you learn about how to cook different foods and become knowledgeable about various recipes, you will also apply these skills as you cook for yourself and your loved ones. Cooking can be an outlet for when you have a lot on your mind, as well. When you are able to focus on the process of making food instead of what is worrying you, you might realize that your problems aren't so bad; the worries will pass.

Website design is another example of a practical hobby. Coming up with different templates and ideas of how you can digitally present a website is a great hobby to take up. Once you become more familiar with it, you can utilize your skills to make a website for yourself that can serve any purpose you'd like. You can also offer to help your friends create a website for their own skills. With any digital hobby, you will likely have access to a broader community. The internet is great at connecting people and allowing you to socialize without feeling as pressured as you would with an in-person encounter.

Chapter 2: Listening Skills

While speaking is one factor in having great social skills, listening is equally important. When you become great at speaking to others, you must remember that you also need to allow others to speak. Speech is a huge form of expression, and you become more likable when you are able to listen to what other people have to say. There are different types of listening actions that you probably utilize every single day without even realizing it. Some situations only call for a listening ear so that a person can vent to you. Other times, the person will want your input. By observing the social cues that you are given, you should be able to differentiate between the two.

The best way to show other people that you are paying attention to them is through active listening. You should be able to demonstrate this by acknowledging what the other person is saying while being free of distractions. If you were to pull out your phone while someone was trying to have a conversation with you, this would come across as rude. Even if you do respect the person very much, it is an act of dismissal when you are not fully paying attention to what they have to say. Do your best to make eye contact with the person and do not allow yourself to lean on distractions as a crutch. While being on your phone might comfort you, it is sending the wrong message to the person you are supposedly listening to.

Some situations will be more casual. You might be listening to a friend talk about her new puppy, and though you might not have to come up with a profound response in return, your listening skills will be an indication of how much you care. Simple thought behind these actions can save you from having misunderstandings. So often, people feel the same way, yet their actions say otherwise. No matter if you are having an in-depth conversation or just catching up with someone who you are close to, be respectful by providing them with your undivided attention. Once you get into this habit, you will notice that others are going to start paying more attention to what you have to say in return.

Passive vs. Active

Going deeper, it is important to learn about the two main types of listening that you can perform—passive and active. As you become more knowledgeable about both, observe the way that you interact with other people. You will likely notice that your listening skills could use some improvement. Again, this does not mean that you are doing anything wrong. Noticing your weaknesses will give you the ability to become better, both for yourself and for those around you that you interact with. It is a chance to take an honest look at the way you present yourself to others and think about how you can become better.

Passive

When you listen passively, you are listening to simply hear information about how you would like to perceive it. You might be very attentive and respectful, but passive listening indicates that you aren't making a true attempt to contemplate what is being said from the speaker's perspective. An example of this comes from hearing about the daily specials at a restaurant. You might be in the mood for some pasta, and while listening to the specials, you are likely going to tune out every other dish that isn't pasta. If someone were to ask you to repeat the information, chances are that you wouldn't be able to. There is a certain disconnect when it comes to passive listening. While it isn't necessarily going to be destructive to your interaction, it might hinder the way that you process the information given to you.

Going off of the above example, imagine that your friend was in the restroom while the specials were being recited. Once they have returned, they might want to know what they were. If you aren't able to recite them because you only listened passively, this shows that you weren't listening to take on the information in its entirety. Instead, you were only listening when it pertains to you and your situation. Even if you do not mean it this way, it can appear that you are being self-serving when you only listen passively. It can quickly become a bad habit once you start applying it toward other areas of your life.

Consider if your friend was going through a tough time deciding on which job offer to choose. While you might passively listen to their struggles, you likely won't be able to give them much input if they ask for your opinion. Passive listening allows you to hear what is being said, but you do not go much further than that. You do not take the situation into account as if it were happening to you, so it is likely that you won't form any strong opinions about it. In this case, you wouldn't be much help to your friend on which job might benefit them more.

When you blindly accept opinions from other people as your own opinion, this is another example of passive listening. It does not allow you to think for yourself on how *you* truly feel about the topic. Instead, it gives you a guideline that someone else stands with that you trick yourself into thinking that you should believe too. Being an independent thinker is an incredibly strong social skill to have. It also makes you a more interesting person to talk to. While you do not want to have disagreements with everyone that you talk to, it is important that you stick to your values. Passive listening skips over this step entirely and does not come with any additional thought processing.

If you find that you often participate in passive listening, you will probably find yourself burdened with will-power issues. You aren't going to feel the need to stand up for what you believe is right or wrong when you are simply going with the flow of the conversation. The right balance must be found here. You can be agreeable without being entirely passive. As you observe your listening skills, keep this in mind. Nothing happens overnight, so do not allow yourself to feel bad if you realize that you take on a passive approach. This can be a safety net for people who struggle with their social skills. Much like any other social habits, passive listening can be corrected and changed for the better.

Active

When you listen actively, you are being mindful of what is truly being expressed. While it is not always necessary to have a response to what the other person is telling you, active listening engages your brain differently. Instead of jumping to conclusions or feeling that you have to agree with an opinion being stated, work on simply absorbing what is being said. Pay attention to the words being spoken as well as nonverbal communication. Watch the person's stance, eyes, and expression. These cues can tell you a lot about how the topic truly makes them feel. For things that are especially difficult to express, the words themselves might not fully represent the feelings.

An example of this is when you know that a friend is having a hard time, yet they tell you that they are fine. The words that they say might reflect this sentiment, but you might notice that they are teary-eyed and shifty due to the weight of what they are going through. Being an active listener will allow you to be there for your friend if they want your support. By truly paying attention to the cues that are being given, a promise of support can be enough to turn their whole day around. Compared to a passive listening situation, you might have missed these cues and continued on like nothing was wrong. This could have potentially led your friend to believe that you do not care.

When there is a problem that needs to be solved, an active listener will find a way to chime in and offer a solution. By paying attention to the details that are being expressed, you will find it easy to come up with ideas on how to solve the given problem. Many people are under the misconception that they do not know how to talk to others when in reality, it is the listening that you must improve on. You will find that talking points become easier when you are actively listening because there are already ideas for you to consider. Being included in conversations this way can do a lot to boost your confidence. The more you are able to participate, the more comfortable you will become with your listening and speaking skills.

When you practice active listening, you are able to stay in peak mental shape. Because your brain is fully engaged in the conversation that you are having, you ensure that you exercise your critical thinking skills and your empathy. This doesn't happen with passive listening because the standards are different. By staying aware and on top of the conversation, you are becoming a part of a high-engagement experience that will allow you to grow as a person.

The next time that you talk to someone, make sure that your active listening skills are engaged. You will probably find that you can identify with the person much more easily, as well as know what you need to say to them. This also puts you in the position to consider new thoughts and ideas. When you listen to other viewpoints, you can often find inspiration that you might want to explore in the future. Overall, there are countless benefits that you will experience as an active listener. Even if you find that you mostly listen in a passive state right now, there are ways that you can transform your skills.

When someone is speaking to you, enter each conversation as though they have something valuable to teach you. Listen intently to what they are saying without passing any prior judgment or suggestions. Allow them to fully express their thoughts before chiming in with your own. If a solution is being sought, do your best to take the words that you were given with all of the non-verbal cues to come up with a response that is both empathetic and understanding. Once you master this, active listening will become second nature to you.

Empathy and Understanding

Simply put, empathy is the ability to stand in someone else's shoes. When you have empathy for a certain situation, you can imagine if it were happening to you. This is an emotionally important skill to have because it allows you to help those around you. When your friends or loved ones come to you for advice, you will be able to consider their experience and understand what they are going through. Empathy brings people closer together; it connects you without having much to be said. As you work on improving your social skills, empathy is definitely one to prioritize.

There are different types of empathy to consider. Some come from natural feelings that you already have, while others are triggered because of the other person saying or doing something. It is fascinating to take a closer look at what allows for this understanding. By doing so, you can actually learn a lot about yourself. The following are some of the most common forms of empathy that you will experience:

1. Affective: This type of empathy revolves around the idea that you can understand someone because you can understand their emotions. For example, if your friend is going through a breakup and starts crying because she misses her ex-partner, you will likely be able to identify with this emotion. When you have this type of understanding, you are able to approach the situation from a place of concern or care.

   What you must be careful of is that you cannot get too emotionally involved in the other person's situation. This might eventually lead you to develop feelings of personal distress because you are able to relate so easily. When we go through things in life, it becomes easier to emotionally identify with others who are experiencing the same things that we have experienced. A careful balance is necessary in order to ensure that you are helping the other person, without hurting yourself in the process.

2. Cognitive: This type of empathy is felt mentally, but not emotionally. It is the ability to allow yourself to think the way that this person is thinking without placing yourself

into their emotional state of being. While it is still a form of empathy, it is more removed than affective empathy because you are simply staying on the outside of the situation.

This can be a great starting point in practicing your empathic skills. When you can listen to someone express a problem and still come up with a few solutions based on the way that they are thinking, it is a skill to be proud of. You will also be more protected because you aren't emotionally involved. Be careful that you do not come across as cold when you express cognitive empathy. Your behavior will be misunderstood if you do not incorporate some warmth in your language or your attitude.

3. Somatic: This is a unique form of empathy because it is physical. This happens when you can identify with someone so strongly that your body has some kind of physical reaction. This can be in the form of a stomachache, for example. If you have ever heard about some bad news, it is likely that you felt it in the pit of your stomach. This is a somatic reaction. It doesn't always have to be a negative response. You can also feel happiness physically. Somatic empathy is a very strong form of empathy that is a great skill to have.

Out of all three forms, this one can become the most bothersome if you allow yourself to feel too much negativity at once. Feelings of sadness, fear, and embarrassment have the ability to weigh you down, even if they are not directly related to you. Know that there is nothing wrong with you or with the way that you function; you are simply in tune with your empathetic side when you can experience these feelings physically.

Whether you have felt all of these or none at all, there is room for you to improve your skills. When you are able to display empathy, you will become a better listener. No matter what type of conversation you are having, you should always be aiming to use your active listening skills. This becomes a lot easier when combined with empathy because you will be able to listen and form your own opinions a lot more quickly. Based on the information that is given to you and your perception of what should be done, your suggestions will be full of valuable advice.

You won't have to worry about or become self-conscious of the way that you interact with others. There is a general misconception in place that people who have social prowess always know the right thing to say. This isn't true! Those who are extremely social might always have something to say, but there is no guarantee that it will be profound or from the heart. By showcasing empathy and active listening to the people that you speak to, you are offering many valuable qualities. People will take notice of this, and they will want to be around you more. It all starts from the very first steps of the way that you present yourself to others in a conversation.

Even if you have these skills, yet you are feeling unsure about what to say in a conversation. Do not feel like you need to fill every single silence. Not all silence is uncomfortable. In fact, it can serve a reflective purpose. Only speak when you feel that you have something relevant to say. This will avoid misunderstandings or filler topics that will not actually benefit the interaction. It is much more desirable to say what you truly feel than what you believe the other person wants to hear. This is an honorable approach that is to be appreciated.

Your empathy and understanding should be utilized, even when you are speaking to somebody that you don't particularly like or identify with. These skills can actually help you form a better bond sometimes. Remember that empathy does not mean that you must agree with the other person and their situation. It is simply a way of showing that you are listening to their experience for what it really is without applying any of your own judgment to it. When you put yourself in their shoes, you might realize that you really aren't very different at all. Certain things can become lost in translation when you put too much focus on reaching the same conclusion. We are different individuals and will form different opinions, but that doesn't mean that we can't get along or be friends.

The next time that you engage in a conversation, observe the type of empathy that you currently hold. By doing so, you will know what you have to work on to become a more well-rounded conversationalist. Communication takes work, but it doesn't have to be difficult. You will probably enjoy all of the new things that you find out about yourself in the process. Know that everyone will have a different starting point, and the point that you are at right now is entirely valid. No single person's influence should be enough to make you feel that you need to change who you are. Instead, you can work with the listening skills that you have, and think about ways in which you can enhance them.

Chapter 3: Conversation Skills

The biggest struggle for anyone who is looking to improve their social skills comes from not knowing how to hold a conversation. There are so many factors involved that have the ability to intimidate you. When you feel intimidated by going into the conversation, you won't be able to show the other person the best parts of you. Instead, you will likely be hiding behind a defense mechanism. In this chapter, you will learn ways for you to comfortably venture out of your shell and feel great about the conversations that you have.

Talking to other people can be scary. When you are unsure of what they will say or how they will react to you, it can cause you to become nervous. This chapter will focus on how you can get over this nervousness and allow yourself to communicate effectively. By working around your shy tendencies and doing things that will allow you to boost your charisma, you will see that you can become great at having conversations. Whether you know the person already or you are talking to a stranger, the confidence that you will feel will be enough to get you through any conversation.

Combat Shyness

If you are ever in a situation where you feel that you have to withdraw from what is going on, you are probably experiencing a certain degree of shyness. Many people experience this. In fact, there are up to 17 million individuals in America alone that feel the same way you do. To know that you aren't alone on this issue can help you to overcome it. By incorporating these strategies into your conversation skills, you will find ways to get past your shyness and actually enjoy talking to other people.

- Act Confident: Whether you are able to feel it or not, it is always great to act more confidently than you feel. By doing so, you are building yourself up and showing other people that you actually do hold this much confidence inside. Even if your voice shakes when you speak, imagine that you are an interesting and charismatic person with a lot to say. After some time, you will start believing this about yourself. The way that you talk to yourself has a huge impact on the way that you are able to talk to other people.

- Participate: When there are conversations that you can become a part of, do your best to participate. Even if you don't have anything new to say, you can still comment on what other people are saying. If you like something that is being said, express this. A simple agreeable remark is great for boosting your conversation skills. The more that you do this, the more you will feel comfortable with contributing new things to the conversation. Don't overwhelm yourself or believe that there are any standards that you must adhere to. Your level of comfort is your only priority.
- Try New Things: It is one of the most common ways to work on your shyness, but that's because it is one of the most effective. Trying new things will allow you to step outside of your comfort zone. If you are tired of feeling a certain way, then you know that something must be changed in order to feel differently. Get out of your routine and try something that has always been of interest to you. Again, this is not about shocking your

system. It is simply so that you can have some new experiences and maybe find some new interests.

- Speak Up: The volume in which you speak says a lot about how you are participating in a conversation. It can be hard, but it is important that you speak clearly and loudly enough so that others can hear you. The last thing that a shy person wants is more attention on themselves in a social setting. If you speak too quietly, then you will be asked to repeat yourself. With a reasonable volume and a steady tone, do your best to speak up when you are a part of a conversation. This will also imply that you are confident and sure of yourself.

- Embrace Vulnerability: Being vulnerable is not a bad thing. It is a natural human emotion that many people feel. Learn to embrace this feeling and accept it. When you try to challenge this, it can make you feel bad about yourself, as if you are not good enough. Don't worry about the amount of vulnerability that you have inside or how often you express it. Any level of expression is normal and valid. The vulnerability can actually be a great quality to have. It normally shows that a person is empathetic and understanding.

- Be Aware of Your Body Language: As you know, communication is done more than just verbally. Your posture can also be a great indicator of how you feel. Just as you must learn how to decipher others' body language, you must be aware of your own. Stand confidently and face the person that you are talking to. Avoid slouching and keep your shoulders back and comfortable. Maintain a relaxed and confident stance. Keep your hands free of any fidgeting if you can help it. This will keep you grounded and show that you are interested in the conversation.

- Practice Mindfulness: Being mindful means that you are taking others into account. When you listen to what is being said and consider where the person is coming from, you might be able to better identify with them. By staying aware of the way that the conversation is flowing, you will likely find it easier to open up to other people. Instead of thinking about all of the ways in which you do not identify with someone, focus on the simple commonalities that you do have. This can be anything from living in the same neighborhood to being born in the same era. You aren't as different from other people as you might think.

Your shyness doesn't have to define you. The traits that you do possess go beyond the fact that you might feel a little shy in social situations. Don't lose sight of these great qualities that you have. It becomes easy to only focus on what you see as your flaws, but these aren't the only things that make you who you are. Know that you are a whole person with valid emotions and interesting ideas. People will enjoy speaking with you, as long as you give them the opportunity to do so.

While it is important to work on expanding your social horizons, know that you do not have to banish your shyness before you can experience great interactions with other people. Work on yourself while you work on stepping outside of your comfort zone. Accept who you are while believing that other people will see the same great qualities that you can see. Every single person has something that they are insecure about, so know that you are not alone in your struggle. Most of the time, people are too busy thinking about their own flaws than paying attention to yours.

Boost Your Charisma and Self-Esteem

When you think about the most interesting person that you know, it is likely you feel this way because they are full of charisma. Your charisma is the energy that you radiate. It has the ability to make people feel a certain way when you walk into the room. The natural charisma that you exude has everything to do with the way you feel about yourself. If you have low self-esteem, it is likely that your charisma needs some work. When you are busy feeling self-conscious, you will likely withdraw slightly. Any charisma that you do possess will be repressed because of your worries of not being accepted.

To improve your charisma and feel better about yourself, there are many ways that you can boost positivity. Starting with the way that you present yourself; it is very important that you amp up your body language. As you know, body language can say a lot about a person. It communicates more than words do, sometimes. Try using your hands more while you speak to further express yourself. Allow your expressions to mimic exactly how you are feeling. People who are able to appear more animated are usually associated with being charismatic. This might be hard for you to master at first because social anxiety has the ability to shrink you. Work on being the most expressive version of yourself that you can be.

When you are having a conversation, try incorporating rhetorical questions. This type of question invokes curiosity from the people around you. It encourages people to think and gives you a way to continue a conversation without trying to carry the weight of it on your own. An example of a great rhetorical question to ask is "what happens next?" It is the type of question that doesn't necessarily require an answer, but it can encourage people to chime in with their theories and ideas. You can also say things such as, "How is everyone doing tonight?" While it is a sincere question, it also goes without saying that you are not counting on every single person in the room to answer it.

After hearing a statement that you identify with, express this by repeating the statement and saying that you feel the same way. This brings a sense of strength to the emotional connection that you have with the person you are talking to. Instead of simply nodding in agreement, being able to identify with them and speak up about it will create a sense of solidarity. A lot of people simply want to be understood, and it is a very validating feeling when someone else can explicitly say that they feel the same way about the same thing that you do.

Share your own personal stories. A charming way to let people in and have them get to know you is by telling a story about something that you have been through. This can be funny or serious depending on the nature of the conversation that you are having, and it is a way for you to show more of who you are to the person that you are talking to. Stories are interesting, and most people love to hear them. This is a great way to talk about yourself when you are uncomfortable about directly listing facts about yourself. Using a story as the structure makes it less formal and easier to communicate. You might find that you truly enjoy this story-telling, and you will be able to utilize it often while you are having conversations.

Rely on your moral conviction to get your point across. If you highly agree with something that is being said, express this and follow up with "because it is the right thing to do." People enjoy talking to others that are sure of themselves. While you still might be working on improving your self-esteem, this is a way for you to express it without coming off as conceited or arrogant. By simply reiterating a point and identifying the moral principle behind it, you are going to grab the attention of others because of your conviction. People with great charisma appear to be sure of themselves at all times. This is a way for you to practice being confident and self-assured.

Set high expectations of the conversations that you have. Instead of focusing on yourself potentially not being good enough, funny enough, or interesting enough, place this focus on the other people who you are speaking with. Without being judgmental, you can have these high expectations when you speak to others. Think about what you'd like to get out of the conversation. Are you aiming to move beyond small talk? Do you want to create a stronger connection? Stick to these expectations and try to guide the conversation in a way that will lead you to these goals. The best thing is that no one else needs to know about your expectations. They can be your own guidelines to utilize as you talk to different people.

The idea behind charisma is that you do not need to try hard to obtain it. Your charisma will find you naturally, and it should be an effortless expression. With time, you will become better at expressing it. To start, you can try some of the above methods when you are having a conversation. This will change things up, and it will also shift the focus onto other things. One of the most nerve-wracking parts of talking to other people is the idea that they are hanging on the edge of their seats, waiting for your reply. The techniques provided take away the pressure of engaging in a conversation while still allowing you to appear interesting and present.

Overcome Your Fears and Insecurities

Your fears and insecurities are what hold you back when you try to talk to other people. While they are all valid to experience, they can become bothersome by hindering you. Sometimes, they can become so powerful that you might feel discouraged from even talking to anyone at all. By following these steps, you can learn how to move past your fears and work through your insecurities:

1. Identify What Hinders You: The first step is to determine what exactly bothers you about talking to other people. It will likely have more to do with the way you feel about yourself than anything to do with the other people. Whether you become so nervous that you stutter or you can't think of anything to say when you have a conversation, your fears are all valid. Name them, and take away their power.

Once you have an idea of what bothers you, dig deeper. Consider why you feel this way. Did you experience something in the past that now impacts your present ability to speak to others? Do the fears only pop up when you are engaged in certain activities? Try to reach the root of the issues. When you have a better understanding of your fears, you will be able to figure out what it takes to move past them, and what you need to help you move past them.

2. Challenge Your Insecurities: Make sure that you realize your insecurities are thoughts that you create. They are interpretations of how you feel about yourself, and luckily, interpretations can be changed. You decide whether you want to believe that you are awkward or whether you want to believe that you are amazing. It takes time to challenge this mindset, so be patient with yourself.

If you'd like to see a change, you need to present a challenge. Think about your insecurities in an objective way, and work toward a goal of moving past them. Visualize the freedom you will feel when you are able to socialize without creating these fears for yourself. By challenging yourself, you will be focusing on the reality of the situation. Doubts might still be present, but you should be able to get to a point of knowing that a change is realistic.

3. Give Yourself Credit: Think about all of the things that you have already accomplished. It is important that you are still giving yourself credit for those things. You know that these accomplishments did not take place overnight or out of thin air. They took hard work, focus, and determination. Consider the nature of your accomplishments. Is it possible that you could accomplish something similar? It helps to remember what you are capable of because this can boost your self-confidence.

Everyone goes through difficulties, yourself included, but this does not mean that you need to be defined by them and hinder yourself from accomplishing what you desire. Work to your own advantage and play to the skills that you possess. When you set realistic expectations for yourself, you are far less likely to become disappointed. All it takes is a better mindset for you to believe in yourself more.

4. Consider Your Circumstances: Once you have your self-confidence in order, you can then think about your present life circumstances. What position are you

currently in to make a change? Will you need to do anything to prepare for this change? With insecurities, they can often make you feel as though the situation is never going to change. You might feel nervous around people, so you settle into that mentality and believe that you will never be able to feel comfortable.

It is also common to lean on the worst-case scenario. Don't do this to yourself; it will only add more stress to your life. Apply some honest effort without holding any judgments against yourself. The thoughts might still pop up in your mind, but ensure that they will not defeat you. Consider what proactive steps that you could take if something did go wrong instead of believing that there is no hope. Also, allow yourself to think about the best-case scenarios. How would you react to those? This balance will lessen the nervous energy that you feel.

5. Talk to Yourself Positively: The language that you use to talk to yourself is super important. If your head is filled with self-deprecating thoughts, you won't feel motivated to try to work on your skills. Be as gentle as you would with yourself as you would with a loved one. Imagine if you were to put your best friend down and berate them for their nervousness. You likely wouldn't do that, so why do that to yourself?

A great rule to follow is the standard of remaining neutral if you cannot think of anything positive. When you eliminate this negative self-talk from your life, you will notice that the pressure of being perfect starts to subside. Know that you are trying your best, and you should be proud of yourself for even desiring to make a change in the first place.

6. Fully Commit: To commit to improving your social skills is something that goes beyond saying it in your head. It is a whole new lifestyle that you must adopt. From the way that you think, feel, and act, your behaviors will have to be adjusted. By turning your back on old habits and replacing them with healthy new ones, you will gradually commit to the things that you want.

   Condition yourself to learn new behaviors that align with the new skills you hope to obtain. If you want to become a more social person, make sure that you are attending more in-person events and giving yourself more opportunities to be around people. Say yes to things that would ordinarily say no to. To do this, mental strength is necessary. When you commit to anything, your mindset needs to be indestructible. You need to have the mental fortitude to see your commitments through.

Chapter 4: Why is Socializing So Difficult?

If the thought of being out in public for long periods of time makes you anxious, you are not alone. Plenty of people find it difficult to socialize, even when they have the desire to be social. There is nothing wrong with you or the way that you operate; some people have a higher level of sensitivity. If socializing drains you, then it is safe to say that you are likely an introvert. A common misconception is that all introverts are shy people who do not wish to leave the house. While you might feel this way sometimes, this is not the correct definition of an introvert.

To be an introvert means that you recharge when you are alone. This is the time when you feel that you can obtain the most energy. Socializing likely drains you because it feels like work for you and can be tasking on your mental and emotional energy. While you might enjoy it very much sometimes, it can still be a lot to handle since it is so draining. You don't necessarily have to be shy to be considered an introvert. Some introverts love talking to people, yet they still become very tired and have the need to retreat once the socialization period is over.

While you do not need to label yourself, it is still important to understand where your behavior is coming from. Being introverted doesn't necessarily change anything about the way that you must condition yourself if you'd like to get better at socializing. Even some extroverts could benefit from the tips that were listed in the previous chapter. Labels won't change anything about you or the way that you feel, but they might allow you some insight for your natural tendencies. This is all a process toward having a better understanding so you can accept yourself.

How to Challenge Your Inner Critic

Knowing how to silence the negativity will help you overcome the way that you are so critical with yourself. By following these basic steps, you will feel more empowered and capable of socializing with others while simultaneously accepting yourself. Getting past this point is a huge accomplishment that you can be proud of. We are all our own worst critics. By changing your inner-narrative, you will find that your thoughts can actually do a lot to empower you when you are not putting yourself down.

1. Develop An Awareness: It can become very easy to ignore what your own thoughts are telling you. When you work on overcoming your oblivious tendencies, your thoughts can actually teach you a lot about why you might be so critical with yourself. Fear of failure usually goes hand-in-hand with a harsh inner critic. By becoming aware of what fuels you, this is your way of taking back the power. Acknowledge why you are the way you are, and work on accepting this as a fact. You do not need to try so hard to change yourself into someone that you think others want to see. Learn to accept your qualities for what they are, and think about what you most admire or love about yourself.

2. Don't Torture Yourself: When you make a mistake or experience failure, it becomes easy to replay these images in your head over and over again. You can drive yourself crazy thinking about the things you wish you had done differently. This is a torturous reminder of reasons to believe that you are not good enough. Get out of this habit as quickly as you can because this is what fuels your inner critic the most. If you make a mistake, learn from the experience and focus on the solution so it doesn't happen again. While it might impact you greatly, that does not mean that it has to hinder you. Accept that it has happened and move forward. When you dwell on the past, it becomes harder for you to focus on what is presently happening and the potential of what could happen next.

3. Pretend You Are Advising a Friend: The advice that you would give to a friend who is being too hard on themselves is likely advice that is very valuable for you to follow. Imagine what you might say to them to ease their worries. Now, say all of those same words to yourself until you believe it. This is a case where repetition can be a great thing. There is no reason why your own advice should not be applicable to yourself, as well. Taking a look at the bigger picture, you will see that there should be no difference in the way that you value your friends

versus the way that you value yourself. Both are equally important.

4. Take a Look at the Facts: Having a persistent inner critic means that you are likely to run into a lot of "what ifs." What if it doesn't go well? What if you embarrass yourself? What if people don't like you? Do not allow yourself to get worked up if there is no concrete evidence that any of these things are true. This will make you feel exhausted before you even begin socializing. Do your best to only look at things that are factual. For example, you have been invited to a holiday party where you will get the chance to meet many new people. Accept this fact for what it is, and do your best to not overthink about what might happen at the party.

5. Replace Critical Thoughts with Realistic Ones: An example of a critical thought is believing that you will never be a great conversationalist. Examine this closely and you will find that this doesn't need to be the conclusion that you come to. Maybe you enjoy having conversations about your favorite television show. You can reframe that statement by acknowledging that you have an interest in talking about TV. This takes your original statement and transforms it into something

positive while still holding onto its true meaning. You can apply this toward anything that you feel overly-critical about. Think about ways that you can keep the statement true while applying it in a more optimistic fashion.

6. Imagine the Possibilities: While it is great to think about all of the positive things that could happen from any given situation, it is unrealistic to believe that things are going to be perfect. Banishing your inner critic is all about balance. You must open yourself up to thinking about the great outcomes as well as those that are unfavorable. While being open to these possibilities, consider that each of them is realistic. Certain situations are beyond your control, however, you do need to deal with them. This is life, and unfavorable circumstances should not rule over your ability to accomplish things. There is always a way to accomplish your goals and dreams. Sometimes you may have to enlist support and help, but there is always a way to accomplish something. In the most gentle way possible, desensitize yourself. This will make it easier for you to accept whatever outcome you receive.

7. **Apply Acceptance and Self-Improvement to Your Life:** There is a huge difference between accepting that you cannot do something and believing that you can work to become better. Wallowing in the things that you cannot do will bring forward feelings of self-pity. Empower yourself by understanding that there is always room for improvement. Nothing will change if you do not believe that a change is possible. If social situations make you uncomfortable, accept this about yourself and challenge yourself to try them again. The more that you experience something, the more familiar and equipped you will be to navigate through it. When you accept your weaknesses, this does not mean you have to hold onto them forever. It means that you can change them if you feel motivated enough.

Your inner critic is only as powerful as you let it become. If you submit to these doubts that you harbor, you won't feel good about yourself. The way that you feel about yourself can either help you or hinder you. Since you are given a choice, wouldn't you rather take the help? When put into simple terms, you might wonder why you were so focused on your inner critic. Know that it is not the easiest thing to overcome, but you already have everything you need to get started.

Acknowledging Disappointment and Failure

While on the topic of acceptance, one of the biggest things that you must work on if you'd like to improve your social skills is the ability to accept disappointment. Whether you disappoint yourself or someone else does, it will happen, inevitably. Life is full of learning experiences, and there is no way to avoid them. In the end, they will make you stronger and wiser about what to do in the future. The way that you handle failure says a lot about the way you feel about yourself. If you have low self-esteem, you are probably quick to blame yourself whenever anything goes wrong. Even when it is not your fault, your first instinct might be to take the blame.

Not only is this unfair to yourself, but it also shows other people that you are easily influenced. Unfortunately, some people can be quick to take advantage of this when they notice it. Being an agreeable person is a great trait to hold, but knowing your limits is important. If you do not have any limits, this is when you will be taken advantage of. You must value yourself enough to know that you do not deserve to take the blame for other people. The only things that you can be responsible for are your own actions and the way that you feel about yourself.

Accept the fact that, no matter how hard you try, you won't be able to control everything around you. While you might adequately prepare to have a great time out at dinner with friends, other people and other situations might still cause you to feel socially anxious. That is simply something that you must learn how to accept. If you let these circumstances that are out of your control cause you to miss out on experiences, then you are not giving yourself a fair chance to try to make the experience better next time. You should be constantly striving to be better, working on self-improvement along the way.

When you do find yourself disappointed in some way, let yourself feel this. Consider how it impacts you, and acknowledge it. Once you have felt it, allow yourself to move on. People often make the mistake of staying within this disappointment for too long. If you linger, you have the potential to put yourself in a situation that is very hard to get out of. There is no reason to prolong your sadness or negativity. It won't do anything productive for you, and it will now allow you to heal any faster. If anything, it will only make you less likely to participate in that activity again. Know that your feelings are valid, but you cannot wallow in them forever.

Strive to be better. The most successful people experience setbacks, much like you do. No one is above them. Take the challenges that you face and turn them into motivation to become better next time. When you are able to face adversity in this way, it is an admirable quality to have. Not only does it display your strength, but it also showcases your resilience. Do not let your setbacks knock you down for too long. Use them to brainstorm ideas for how you'd like to handle things differently from now on. Disappointment and failure are universal feelings. There is nothing that you can do to avoid them, so you might as well embrace them.

Make it a habit to take action. When you come up with an idea of how you can become better, apply it immediately. You'll see one of two outcomes--the solution will make you stronger, or you will have to head back to the drawing board to try a different one. There is no clear cut answer to what it is going to take to see a difference. You will have to take a trial and error approach in order to find which solution is going to work best for you. During this time, you will likely learn a lot about yourself and what you are most responsive to. Find what motivates you and use it to your own advantage.

The steps that you take to improve your self-esteem will also improve your ability to handle failure. If you feel great about the person that you are, then you won't be so hard on yourself should a failure occur. All of these skills that you will learn are inner-connected, hence making you a better person in all areas of your life. Working on your self-esteem should only be done for one purpose—because you want to do it. No one else can convince you that you need a boost in self-esteem. This is something that you have to decide for yourself because you are the only one who can feel it.

Think about people who inspire you. They can be people you know or people you have seen in the media. Consider who you would like to model your behavior after. Those who are successful definitely understand what failure feels like. Hear their stories and take note of what they did in order to get past their setbacks. When you feel uninspired, it helps to try something completely different. Utilize some of the methods that you read about, and see how you can apply them to your own life. You might be surprised to find that they help you more easily than anything you've tried in the past. Because you know that these people are successful know, you know that the methods truly work.

Know that you are going to have great days and then you might have days where you feel that nothing is going right. Anything bad will not stay that way forever. As long as you believe that you can get up and try again, you will not be phased by any number of setbacks that you experience. One day, your own personal victories might be inspirational to other people. Having a great attitude is contagious, and it helps people more than you know. Not only will you be overcoming your own personal obstacles, but you will also be guiding others through theirs.

Understanding the Difference Between Assertive and Aggressive

Talking to someone who has assertive energy can be very intimidating. When a person is assertive, this means that they radiate a certain and forceful energy. People with this quality are very sure of themselves; they normally don't take no for an answer. When you are socially anxious, speaking to someone like this can cause you to doubt yourself. It is a huge contrast when you mix an assertive individual with a reserved individual. This energy does not have to make you self-conscious, though. You can actually learn from it and use it in order to make the conversation flow continuously. What you must remember about assertive people is that they usually have good intentions. They are not looking to hurt you, but simply to get what they want.

It can be hard to understand someone with this personality because it is likely very different from your own. Different does not have to indicate better or worse. Try not to think about it in those terms. Simply observe and try to accept the person for who they are. Much like you, they have their own unique ways of communicating with other people. While assertive people are socially known as people who have plenty of confidence, there are moments when it can waiver. They are only human, so it is bound to happen. Be sensitive to this possibility.

A person who is assertive will appreciate being heard. When someone wants to express their needs and desires to you, the best thing that you can do is practice your active listening skills. Do not feel pressured to chime in or agree with them if you do not know exactly what to say. Listening is enough, and it is a valuable response. If anyone is that adamant about how they feel, they probably want you to ask them why they feel that way. Ask questions that allow them to further express themselves. By doing so, you show them that you are listening and that you care about what they have to say. A common misconception is that you need to match their energy level. If you are not feeling as high energy, you don't need to pretend that you are. This won't be authentic to your own personality.

It is important that you stay true to your own values and morals. If a person is being so assertive to the point that you feel uncomfortable, it is okay to express an opinion that is different. Just as you were willing to listen to them, a good conversation needs to have a mutual level of acceptance. Talking to someone that you do not necessarily agree with is an enriching experience. It really allows you to acknowledge the way that you personally feel, and it challenges you to accept these parts of yourself. As you have been working to accept who you are, this interaction will allow you to practice being comfortable with your own thoughts and ideas.

Aggressive behavior might appear to be the same thing as assertive behavior at first. The main thing to look out for is the person's intention. If you notice that a person is being assertive, yet they are being too forceful or demanding, this can be an indication that you are actually dealing with an aggressive personality type. This is likely one of the interactions that has the potential to make you feel nervous or unsure of yourself. Aggression happens when there are unresolved feelings involved. Whether the person is actually angry with you or just lashing out at you, know that you are not responsible for the way they speak or behave toward you; chances are they need to sort out what they are feeling.

You have every right to end an interaction that is harmful to you. Whether you are being threatened physically or emotionally, your response is valid. If something just isn't right about the way that a conversation is headed, know that you need to value yourself more than you value hurting someone's feelings or angering them further. Calmly talk about how you feel without placing any blame on the other person. The worst thing you can do to an aggressive person is to challenge their feelings. In the best way that you are able to, try to bring the conversation to an endpoint. Some examples of this can look like the following:

"I understand where you are coming from. This is how I feel."

"I'm unsure of my opinion on this."

"I'll have to give this some more thought before I'm able to share my own opinion."

These are all ways that provide social cues to the other person that you'd like to stop talking about whatever you are talking about. Without being rude or demeaning to them, you will also be protecting yourself. Unfortunately, aggression can show up unexpectedly. You might know someone very well, and then you will get to see a different side of them that you haven't seen before. Regardless of the capacity in which you know the person, remember that you have the right to feel the way that you are feeling. Many people freeze up during aggressive situations because they do not want to make them worse. This is definitely something to be careful of. Instead of submitting to the behavior, you can do your best to redirect it instead.

Again, there is no need for you to feel bad about not agreeing with the way that another person is acting. If you truly cannot identify with them, you do not need to lie or sacrifice your own morals in order to conform. When you do this, it is easy to lose track of who you are as a person. Your values are far more important than having a desire to please everyone that you interact with. Know that it is impossible to please everyone. When you try to do this, it will only stress you out and potentially make you feel bad about yourself.

Chapter 5: Good Manners

When speaking with anyone, good manners will always be recognized. This goes for both yourself and the person you are interacting with. Having good manners becomes synonymous with being kind. The idea of having a conversation with a kind person sounds a lot less intimidating than talking to someone who is known for being rude. Manners are also an indication of your level of selflessness. When you are willing to be there for someone without interrupting them, this shows that you truly care about what they are experiencing. Those with no manners will normally act in the entirely opposite way. A selfish person would not be phased by interrupting someone else. It is important that you are able to recognize these crucial differences.

Your manners are what makes your first impression for you. If someone perceives you as polite, then they will likely want to interact with you again. A lot of the time, when someone does not seem to like you after a conversation, this is because you gave off a bad first impression. While you can't necessarily control what others are going to think of you, nor should you, it does help when you make an effort toward being a great person. Learn how to apply good manners to daily conversations. This will allow people to see that you are a great person who is great at interacting.

You were probably taught manners during childhood. From the basics of saying 'please' and 'thank you' to conversation skills, it can be easy to forget these things as you develop habits as an adult. Unfortunately, manners are normally one thing that can get left behind. If you notice that your skills are lacking, you should make it a priority to re-learn them. Your manners will take your social skills to a new level, and they will allow you to make the best first impression that you can.

While manners do include basic kind actions such as opening doors for other people and sending out thank you cards, they extend beyond this concept. To truly have good manners means that you always take into consideration how others are feeling.

While writing a thank you card can be a polite gesture, if you know that someone prefers to hear your voice, give them a call. This is a small action that you can do that will please the other person while also improving your manners. As you can see, both parties will benefit from actions like these.

By practicing good manners, you are setting the standard for the kind of social interactions that you would like to have. It can be unnerving to think about all that can happen during social interaction, but in a way, expressing good manners give you some control. You can utilize your manners in order to show other people that you are expecting the same kind of treatment in return. Others will be more willing to give you respect when you are already showing them the same respect. Many social interactions rely on reciprocation. If you are too stubborn to be nice or polite, waiting on the other person to display these actions first can backfire on you. By holding out on your good manners, the other person can develop a skewed perception of who you are.

Consider that each culture has a different set of acceptable social norms. What might be considered polite to you is perceived differently by someone who grew up within a different culture. When you are unsure of what is polite and impolite, it is best that you simply ask. If you are doing something that appears to make someone uncomfortable, express that it is not your intention to do so. After this, you can find out if your actions are indeed considered impolite and then you can change them. It is better to ask outright than be left to wonder what you are doing wrong.

Table manners are a subset of manners that are also essential to your social skills. No matter where you are eating, there is a certain standard of etiquette that should be followed. These manners are optional, but showing the initiative to use them shows that you care about how others around you might feel. The first step is to sit properly while maintaining eye contact with those who talk to you at the table. If you are slouching with your elbows propped up, this gives you an attitude that suggests you do not care to be polite.

If you need something, ask a person beside you or across from you to pass it to you. Reaching over other people while they are eating is considered very rude. If most of the table is seated, but you are still waiting on some others, it is polite to wait until everyone is there before you start eating. Chew with your mouth closed, and refrain from talking until your mouth is empty. Keep your napkin on your lap and use your utensils. When you master your table manners, you will be able to make a great first impression at any gathering or event.

The do's and don'ts of having good manners is not a hard concept to grasp. As long as you can remain aware of the way that you are behaving, then you should be able to present your best self to those you interact with. Overall, having a pleasant expression on your face will be a foundation for you. No matter how rudely someone behaves with you, keeping a pleasant or neutral expression will prevent you from getting into altercations. While you might not agree with what is being said, it is polite to not get into heating confrontations with other people. Use your conversation skills to express your opinions clearly, instead.

Treat other people the way that you hope to be treated. Even if someone is displaying bad manners toward you, this should not impact the way that you behave. Keep your composure, remain aware of your body language, and try not to let the bad attitudes of other people keep you from holding onto your great social skills. Not everyone will hold themselves to the same standards of manners as you will, but this is okay. This does not prevent you from trying to be the most polite and caring individual that you can be.

Why They Are Important

Manners are important because they help you get along with other people. With any social interaction, you can probably conclude that your goal is to get along with that person. It doesn't feel great when you just cannot see eye-to-eye with someone. You can avoid having experiences like these by ensuring that you are properly displaying your manners. When you can get along with anyone, you will have an easier time starting conversations. The fear of not knowing what to say will not hold you back. Manners give you a way to maintain an easy-going attitude.

Kindness is encouraged when good manners are expressed. There is a lot of hatred that unavoidably exists in the world already, so there is no reason that you need to contribute to it. When you exemplify kindness and grace, other people will inevitably notice you. They might reconsider the way their behavior because you are showing them that they can be kind instead. This kind of impact is a great one to have, allowing others to redefine their own social skills.

On a professional level, having good manners can land you a job. One of the main traits that employers look for in a person is their ability to get along with others and to be polite. In most work settings, you will need to work as a team to complete goals. If you cannot get along with the other members of your team, this doesn't only come across as rude, but it jeopardizes the company because the work isn't being completed. Employers are known to look at the bigger picture, gauging how you will fit in with the other team members.

When you do get called in for a job interview, remember to treat the person who is interviewing you with respect. Showcase your best manners during the interview process. This person will likely be your supervisor, so if there is ever a time to make a great impression, this is it. When you get into the habit of regularly displaying your good manners, it becomes second nature to do so. You won't even have to think twice about it while you are being interviewed because the conversation will go just like any other conversation that you have.

Just as important as your professional life is your home life. The members of your household deserve the same amount of respect as any of your employers. It can be easy to let the manners slip while you are at home. For one, you might feel more comfortable at home, so this encourages a more casual attitude. While this is okay, you must never let your manners slip so that you begin expressing things in a rude way. An example of this would be if you need to use the bathroom, but it is occupied. While it might be tempting to bang on the door until your family member comes out, this is incredibly rude.

Your romantic relationship will benefit from a display of good manners. When couples disagree with one another, it becomes way more chaotic than it needs to when the manners are dropped. Just because you are angry or frustrated does not mean you should lose sight of these things. Keeping your composure will benefit both yourself and your significant other. It will keep you both on track so that you can work through the issues that you are having without getting caught up on one nuance. Nobody likes to argue, and displaying good manners can assure that you will spend less time doing it.

Consider the feelings that you might get when you are driving on the road and someone cuts you off. This will likely send many people into a fit of rage. Road rage is a very real issue that can evolve into something much worse if you are not careful. While it might feel great to blast the horn and speed around this person who wronged you, do not forget that your safety is being put at risk when you begin driving erratically. Your manners can help your road rage. Sure, there are incidents that happen that are incredibly frustrating. You have every right to feel this way. Taking on a personal vendetta, however, will not make matters any better. Consider the consequences of your actions.

Your reputation is something that you need to consider. No matter what social situation you become involved in, each instance is a chance for you to develop a great reputation. When you have this, people will learn about who you are and remember that they enjoy being around you. This can lead to more invitations and more interactions in the future. If you do not make it a point to express your good manners during social situations, you will become known for this. Once the word gets around, you might find that people have been avoiding you because of this. No one enjoys being berated or flat-out disrespected. Make sure that you take as much pride in your reputation as you should.

Now that you are familiar with the many ways that your manners can help your social skills, you should be feeling motivated to craft your skills. As you are working toward being more polite, you are going to want to practice this frequently. This means that you will be seeking out more social interactions so that you have a chance to do so. Enjoy this process because it will teach you a lot. You might have to try many different methods before you find the ones that work best for you. While you do not have to be over-the-top with your manners, you must gauge each situation and then determine what the most appropriate level is in order to display them. Play each instance by ear. No two situations are going to be exactly alike.

Ways That Manners Are Forgotten

As you experience more things throughout your life, it becomes easier to let your manners slip. When you were a child, you likely had a parental figure to oversee the way that you were acting. This means that you got reminders to be polite and helpful tips in order to make sure that you were being respectful. As adults, we no longer have these constant reminders. It becomes your own responsibility to keep track of your own behavior. Make it a point to actively remind yourself that your manners impact how you are perceived and treated. If you want to be great at socializing, then you need to care about the way you come across to other people.

The more comfortable you feel with a person, the easier it becomes to let your manners slip as well. For those that you live with or those that you have known for a long time, you might be a little bit lax with your display of manners. While this can be okay, you need to make sure that you do not drop your good manners altogether. No matter how close you are to someone, they also deserve your respect. Too much joking around can create bad habits that you might be prone to relying on. As a general rule, speak to others the way you would like to be spoken to. While you might not feel the need to greet your best friend with a handshake, they do deserve your eye contact and undivided attention. Use your best judgment.

Being treated poorly can impact the way that you treat others. If you have encountered rude people in the past, these experiences might shape the way you express yourself. It doesn't feel good to be wronged, but having a vindictive mentality will not help the situation. It will only make you hardened and less able to express yourself in polite ways. Use these situations as learning experiences that are here to guide you toward better choices. Think about the way that you were treated, and know that you wouldn't want to treat other people in that way. You can gain inspiration from these moments, ones that guide you toward better life decisions.

You might come to the realization that you have people in your life who constantly treat you poorly. This is a case of toxicity that can be hard to deal with when you don't know what to do. There are times when having a person like this in your life will force you to make a tough decision—do you deal with this person's behavior or cut them out of your life entirely? Know that removing someone from your life is an entirely personal decision, but if you notice that the person is a bad influence on you, then you should not have to put up with it. Cutting ties with someone can be intimidating, but if it will make your life better, then know that you should not feel selfish for doing it.

Below are some ways that you can get back on track with your manners. You can apply these tips toward your daily life while taking note of the way that each one makes you feel. It is likely that you will notice other people start treating you differently the more polite than you are.

- Say Please and Thank You: This is one of the most basic behavioral habits to get back into, yet many of us forget this simple act of kindness. This display of polite behavior can make a big difference in the way that others perceive you. Saying please and thank you allows the other person know that you are grateful and that their efforts are being appreciated. It is something very simple, but the impact that it makes will remind you of the benefits of having good manners.

- Ask Before Assuming: No matter what the situation is, it is always better to ask before you assume that you can take action. An example of this would be if a friend were eating and you wanted a bite. While you might be friendly with one another, it can feel natural to just reach over and grab some of their food. The polite thing to do, however, is to ask if you can have some. This establishes your respect for them while also being direct with what you want.

- Make Eye Contact: When you are not used to holding direct eye contact with people, it can be a challenge. Eye contact is important because it shows the other person that you are actively listening. If your eyes begin to wander while you are in the middle of a conversation, this gives off the impression that you do not care about what is being said. While you do not need to stare into the other person's eyes, do make an effort to maintain some eye contact. This will keep you engaged in the conversation and focused on what to say next.

- Participate in Random Acts of Kindness: You do not need a reason to do something nice for someone else. If you want to practice your kindness, do so because you feel it in your heart. This can be a great reminder to the other person of how much you care about them. It also feels good to be nice. Your own mood will be uplifted as you intend to lift the moods of others. The more kindness that you are able to spread, the happier your interactions will make people.

- Treat Others the Way You Want to Be Treated: You have likely longed for acceptance within social settings. Being unsure of yourself can be very difficult, especially when you feel that you are alone in the struggle. When you do have the opportunity to talk to people, it doesn't make sense to be anything less than polite. The way that you treat other people will be directly reciprocated in the treatment that you receive in return. Imagine your ideal social situation, and treat people the way that you hope they will treat you.

Chapter 6: Body Language

Your spoken language isn't the only way you can express yourself. Body language is a language that everyone speaks; it is universal. Whether you can't control yourself because you are happy or your body showcases that you are feeling sad, body language is a very important cue for others to follow. The importance of body language is often overlooked because it can be a very subtle form of communication. Most of the time, you probably aren't even aware of your body language. In this chapter, we will take a look at the different ways you can express yourself by using your body, facial expressions, and hand gestures. You will learn how people perceive you and how you can interpret them in return.

Body language comes from more than just your body. It can also be observed by how much (or how little) you use your hands while you speak, the ways that you stand, and the expressions that you pair with what you are saying or reacting to. Know that other people are likely going to notice your body language before you do. It is the way you are presenting yourself to others. For this reason, awareness is important. If you feel constantly awkward, yet you seem to have conversation skills mastered already, there could be a divide between what you are saying and what you are portraying.

Working from the top down, think about the way that your eyebrows can control a conversation. You might have thought of your eyebrows as unimportant before, but they actually have a lot of control over your facial expressions as a whole. Raised eyebrows can indicate skepticism or surprise. A furrowed brow can showcase sadness or disappointment. A slight lift might mean that you are feeling happy or peaceful. There are so many different ways that your eyebrows can match up with the conversation that you are having. Be aware of the way that you hold them because they can let the other person in on how you are feeling.

Directly below your eyebrows, your eyes can say a lot about you. When you refuse to make eye contact with someone that you are talking to, think about the way that this will come off to them. They might take it as a sign that you are not interested, or that you do not respect what they have to say. Even if neither of these things is true and you might just be nervous, avoiding eye contact entirely is one of the biggest social mistakes that you can make. Even if you cannot maintain constant, direct eye contact, you should still try to make an effort to get in a few moments where your eyes meet the other person's. Working on this will allow it to get better over time.

The mouth is arguably the most important part of your body when it comes to communication, and this is not even including the fact that this is how you speak. Think about the power behind a smile. This can take a conversation from intimidating to comfortable. If you are feeling happy, let the other person know. Smile at them, and if you do not feel like smiling, do your best to keep your mouth relaxed and slightly upturned. Even the most minimal instance of a frown can completely change the mood of the conversation. If you are feeling upset, then you can't help frowning or grimacing. But if you are feeling good, let it be known that your mouth should match. Practice speaking in front of a mirror to work on your charisma. Talk about a range of different topics. You can really pay attention to your facial expressions this way.

Your posture comes next. Believe it or not, the way you stand can say a lot about how you are feeling. A general rule of thumb is to keep your posture open and relaxed when you are speaking to someone. Face the person directly, maintain eye contact, and keep your arms down at your side. The main indication that you are unhappy or uncomfortable comes from crossing your arms over your chest. Crossed arms are the universal symbol for not being content. Even if you feel perfectly fine, you might still be in the habit of doing this. Work on ways that you can feel comfortable without crossing your arms. Lean up against a surface if you have to, but ensure that you are still facing the person that you are talking to.

As mentioned, the way that you hold your arms matters to the overall feeling of the conversation. Understandably, fidgeting or folding your arms might happen naturally as a defense mechanism. If you aren't great at having conversations yet, they will probably still make you feel nervous. Fidgeting can be distracting, and even though you might be expressing your words clearly, the other person might not be able to grasp what you are saying if you keep fidgeting in front of them. When you know that you are going to be in a social setting, expend that nervous energy ahead of time if you can, this way you won't fidget while in a social setting. Use fidget cubes and other devices to release the nervous energy you feel. Learn how to be comfortable with the idea of keeping your arms uncrossed and relaxed as you speak.

Hand gestures can be a great addition to a conversation once you get the hang of them. They can be used to add to what you are trying to say. Talking with your hands is an animated way to further enforce your point. Whether you are excited or naming things from a list, your hands might naturally want to move to the words that you are saying. As long as you are not fidgeting, explore these hand gestures and allow this to happen. Moving your hands is natural, and if they can help you express yourself, they are a great social skill to take on. Do not feel that you *have* to use hand gestures because this will only become awkward. Use them if you feel the urge to, but if not, you can save them for when you are feeling more comfortable.

Your legs are the final aspect of body language to be aware of. There isn't really much that you can do with your legs during a conversation, but there isn't much that you need to do. Shuffling around a lot is a clear indication of nervousness. If you want to appear as self-confident as possible, stand still. There is no need to walk around or move when the other person isn't doing the same thing. Take their social cues into consideration while you talk to them. Moving your legs and feet only makes you feel increasingly uncomfortable even though it is another defense mechanism. Do your best to be comfortable with just standing still.

Consider that your body language might be different when you are sitting versus when you are standing. The same basic principles still apply, but there are a few additional things to be considerate of. If you are sitting at a table with someone, it is considered impolite to place your elbows on the table. If you need to place anything on the table, only rest your hands there. Especially if you are in a setting where you will be eating, having your elbows on the table is a sign of disrespect. Sit up tall and straight; any type of slouching or leaning can come across as impolite, as well. Eye contact might be easier to maintain at a table setting because you might be talking to more than one person at a time. Divide your eye contact equally, slightly turning to face who you are addressing each time.

Think about the way that you greet someone when you first meet them. Do you stand before them and wave or do you shake their hand? In general, a handshake is an indication that you are respectful and confident. Work on your handshake, ensuring that it is not too loose but also not too firm. Make eye contact during the handshake, and don't forget to smile. This is the first impression, and you know how important it is to make a lasting first impression. Treat yourself how you would hope to be treated, providing the other person with an attitude that is warm and inviting.

It sounds like there is so much to remember when it comes to body language, but it isn't difficult when you pay attention to the cues that your body naturally makes. It is likely that you already have your own physical traits that you aren't even fully aware of yet. As long as you have this basis, then you can improve upon it. Take note of the way that you present yourself while you are speaking to other people, and ask yourself what you can do to make the interaction even better. Practice the above tips to become great at the way that you show your body language.

Practical Application

Learning about new skills is great, but being able to apply them to your real life is even better. That is the goal with the guide. Not only should you be retaining these concepts, but you should be able to find ways to incorporate the tips into your life. To work on your body language skills, start by observing. This is one of the best ways to learn how to get better at something. Not only should you be observing your own behavior, but pay attention to the ways that other people express their own body language. Now that you are familiar with all of the different movements, you can take a look at the way that others choose to portray themselves. It is likely that you will learn a lot from this simple observation.

Think about the most charismatic people that you know. Why do you feel this way about them? The traits that they display are going to be a great starting point to model your own behavior after. Pay attention to how they showcase their body language. What do they do that leads you to believe that they excel at communication? To start, observation is all that you really need to do in order to apply practical applications of body language to your own life. The more that you know about the various social cues, the more that you will be able to model your own behavior to fit the specific mood of each conversation that you have.

Practicing standing in front of the mirror while you recite a speech is also a great way for you to observe yourself. Standing before a mirror, read a piece of literature that takes you at least one minute or more. Look at the way that you are standing and what your body language is saying. Sometimes, being able to see exactly what it is that you need to correct can help you to do it easier. Does anything about your stance look awkward? Are you remembering to make occasional eye contact? All of these small things matter; they make up the overall picture of your body language communication.

The next step you should take is having conversations with friends or loved ones that you are very close to. While applying the principles that you have learned, make sure that you are successfully using your body language to convey what you are trying to say. It is often easier to practice new social skills on those that you are familiar with than to try them out for the first time on strangers. When you allow yourself to build up confidence ahead of time, you will have fewer encounters that leave you feeling embarrassed or unsure of yourself.

An interesting concept about becoming great at reading others' body language is that you can actually begin to notice when people are lying to you. When people lie, their body language is normally a dead giveaway. Eye contact becomes flighty, possibly non-existent. If you notice that someone is looking away from you a lot during a conversation, this could be an indication of guilt or nervousness. Taking this into consideration, you can see why it is important that you remain aware of your own levels of eye contact because they can be misunderstood. Shifting in stance frequently can also be an indication that a lie is being told. Lies generally make people feel uncomfortable, whether they realize it or not. A person who is lying will likely have a hard time standing still.

The intention behind the words that are being said is amplified by the way that you pair them with body language. If you want someone to know that you care about them, you should express it in more ways than one. With the words that you say and the actions that you perform, you will become more comfortable with this type of expression. If you feel upset with someone, you can also apply the same concepts by pairing your verbal language with your body language. You do not always have to censor yourself for the sake of making others feel more comfortable. If you are truly struggling, then you have the right to let the person you are talking to know this.

Body language can help you express the exact emotions that you are feeling. A common struggle with social skills is feeling like you do not know what to say or do. By utilizing body language, you are giving yourself more options. When you have these ways to express yourself, you will be less likely to get stuck without knowing how to continue the conversation. Listen to how you are truly feeling, and let the expression form from there. Be clear with what you need to express, and take a few moments to think about how you would like others to perceive you.

A great trick to utilize is the mirroring trick. As you explore the different ways that you can express yourself, you might need some practice before you feel fully comfortable. In times like these, it actually becomes helpful to simply mirror the other person's energy and body language. If someone is standing openly in front of you and smiling, you can do the same. This is a great tip to utilize that will keep you on track during conversations. If you are ever unsure of how to feel or act, take a look at what the other person is doing and do your best to try to relate to this. Your empathic skills will come in handy for this.

Not only can mirroring help put you at ease when you don't know what to say or do next, but it can also put the other person at ease. It can be nerve-wracking to explain yourself, no matter how comfortable you are with socializing. Mirroring provides a sense of knowing, a sense that no further explanation is needed. This is a powerful tool that strengthens your bond with the opposite person. When they feel like you are on the same page as them, they will naturally feel more comfortable talking to you. This is the start of a great social relationship. Each time you speak to this person, you will be able to grow your bond even more.

Taking a look at the other side of the mirroring technique, if you notice that someone is mirroring you, this means that your energy is strong. This is a great thing because the other person is acknowledging that you appear comfortable and confident in the conversation. When others mirror you, it is a sign of respect. It also shows that they are interested in who you are as a person and what you have to say. Feeling that you have the upper-hand in this way can be a great confidence boost, especially when you were unsure of your social skills to start off with.

When you are speaking to someone, it is important that you are aware of personal space. One way to make someone uncomfortable during a conversation is by standing too close to them. While you might not intentionally do this, you can usually tell by a person's body language if they feel their personal space is being intruded on. Stepping backward is a clear sign that a person is uncomfortable. If you are having a conversation and you notice the person is backing up, do not close the distance again. This body language suggests that they might need some more space. When someone does this, it does not mean that you have done anything wrong. We all have different boundaries when it comes to our own personal space.

In the same way that you must be mindful of others' personal space, make sure that you are comfortable in your own. Backing up can be a useful way to send a hint to that person that you need more space. You can also use objects to create more distance between you, such as a table. It is understandable that your personal space is important to you because that can really impact your ability to socialize. Do not feel weird or guilty if you need more of it than the average person. Your feelings on the matter are valid, and it is up to you to set those social boundaries.

As you know now, body language is a whole other language in itself. It is a way to be expressive without even saying a word. Utilizing clear body language cues can really help you in social situations. They can take things to the next level and make you seem more interested and engaged. Do not forget about your body language while you are socializing with others, and do not forget to observe the body language of the person or people you are interacting with. Both will be beneficial in helping you succeed in social situations.

If social interactions in the past have not gone as well as you had hoped, then you were probably forgetting to be aware of your body language. Practice in the mirror as much as you need until you feel confident in your abilities. There is no set amount of time for how long it takes to master the art of becoming great at using body language. Much like any other social skills you will develop, practice is what will take you to the next level of communication. The best time to start utilizing these skills is right now. There is no need to wait until you feel that they are perfect because there is no such thing as perfect. Socialization is subjective, and you never know what kinds of conversations you will find yourself a part of. The best way to learn is by doing.

Chapter 7: How to Meet New People

As you become more comfortable with your social skills, you will likely have the desire to meet new people. This is a great point to reach because this is when your social life can get the most interesting. By meeting new people, you will be learning a lot. It is thought that the people you interact with influence the way that you live your life. Through their influence, you might learn some new skills and find out even more things that you are interested in. You might be wondering, what is the best way to meet new people and start new friendships? The answer will differ based on your interests. Starting with what you enjoy, it makes sense to seek out people who have common interests.

By now, you know that talking to people becomes easier when you have something to talk about. You reach this point by seeking out those who care about the things that you care about. In this chapter, we will breakdown all of the skills necessary in order for you to create new connections and talk to anyone you want to. Think about the things that you enjoy doing the most. What do you spend your free time on? Through these activities, you can join communities that are filled with other people like you.

If there is a class for something that you enjoy doing, sign yourself up! A learning environment is a great way to bond with other people who are going to be on your level. Because you not only have the activity in common, but you will also have the desire to learn more in common, you can create bonds with other people that allow you both to grow. If you cannot locate classes in your area, consider simply hanging out in public places. Bring a book or a sketchpad to a park, and observe your surroundings. When you notice people around you, each person should provide you with a certain energy. By gauging their energy and watching their body language, you should be able to determine if they want to converse with you.

Interacting with strangers can be intimidating, but think about it this way—what do you have to lose? The worst thing that can happen is the person won't be interested in having a conversation. In this case, simply move on and accept that not everyone is required to be your friend. This does not reflect poorly on the person you are, but it does encourage you to have thicker skin. As you become better at reading people, you will be able to probably guess if someone is open to a conversation or not. As long as you do not take each interaction personally, you will likely begin to enjoy the process of talking to new people without any idea of what is going to happen next.

Confidence

Much like any other social interaction, you need to utilize your confidence, it is a muscle that needs to be exercised daily. Think about the way that you want to present yourself to new people. The best part is that you can portray yourself in any way that you desire because these people do not know you yet. Before you try talking to them, determine which of your strengths you would like to showcase. From the first chapter, you learned how to explore these parts of yourself and to determine what things you like most about yourself. If you can recognize your strengths, other people will also take notice. This is why confidence will get you far when you begin socializing.

Know that when you are interacting with someone new, you should not place strict standards on yourself because the other person isn't going to either. A common mistake we make when meeting new people is being too hard on ourselves when the other person doesn't even feel the same way. Relax and accept the interaction for what it is meant to be. If you start by putting yourself down, you will be miserable by the time you try to start the conversation. This can cause you to appear uncomfortable, and it might bring back those feelings of shyness and nervousness that you have worked so hard to overcome.

Speak clearly and at a reasonable volume. Sometimes, nerves can cause you to forget certain social skills. Speaking too loudly or mumbling can cause the other person to feel uncomfortable. Consider where you are currently located. Are you indoors or outdoors? Are there other people around or are you alone? Use your best judgment to decide on what volume and topics are going to be best. Start with something lighthearted. It is never a good idea to delve into the deeper topics in the beginning because you should work on getting to know the person better first.

A compliment or a nice statement can be a nice way to engage in a conversation for the first time. Without crossing any boundaries, simply pay the person a compliment that you truly mean. If this part is forced, you aren't going to be interacting in a genuine way. If the person responds well to what you are saying, then you can take this as a cue to continue the conversation. You can either continue on the same topic or change it up. This gives you the upper-hand to take the conversation where you would like. If the person reacts coldly to your initial compliment, then you can take this as a cue to end the conversation. This still puts you in a great position because you expressed something that you believe is true, and you tried to put yourself out there socially.

No matter what the outcome is, you will be able to walk away knowing that you were confident enough to try. On the topic of confidence, you will also be building this up for the other person when you pay them a compliment. Even if they do not want to fully engage in a conversation, you can still walk away knowing that you did a kind thing. The interesting part about talking to new people is that you can take the interaction as far as you want it to go. You might make a lifelong friend, or you might simply gain another acquaintance. The more that you grow your social circle, the more that you will be able to work on your newfound social skills.

If you make it a point to express your self-confidence all the time, anywhere you go will become an opportunity to meet new people. You will find that people flock to you when you open up your energy to this type of interaction. Compared to how you felt when you acted in a more reserved manner, you will see that it is actually possible to find a different kind of happiness from putting yourself out there. Even if nothing comes of it, you are still showing other people the best version of yourself, and that is an accomplishment alone.

Talking to Strangers

Talking to strangers does not need to come along with a judgmental label. While some people might find it weird or bizarre, know that talking to strangers is a great way to meet new people and create connections. If you have a desire to talk to someone, as long as it doesn't hurt anyone in the process, you should go for it! Starting with confidence, think about your reason for wanting to approach this person. Do they share common interests with you? Are you simply intrigued to talk to them? Do you find something physically attractive about this person? No matter what your reasoning is, know that it is good enough and you are good enough.

There is an element of surprise that exists when you talk to strangers. You likely weren't planning on doing it, and the other person might have never expected you to approach them. Surprises can be fun and exciting, so you should treat them that way. Keeping the conversation and mood light, explore your compatibility with this person. Do you like the way that they respond to you? While your first attempt to start a conversation is going to be their first impression of you, their reply will also be your first impression of them. Take this into consideration before you decide if you'd like to continue having a conversation or not.

If the two of you hit it off, then this is great! Talk until you feel that you have gotten what you hoped for out of the conversation. As you go to leave, this would be the time when you decide if you'd like to talk to this person again in the future. Some interactions are only meant to be temporary. You might talk to people that you will never see again in your life. If you know that you would like to see this person again though, ask for a way to contact them. Whether you want to ask for their phone number, email address, or social media handle, don't forget to do this before you walk away. If asking is too nerve-wracking, you can start by giving them your information. This gives them the *option* to contact you again if they feel the same way, and it can be a low-pressure way of expressing that you would like to talk again.

Assuming you do receive a way to contact this person again, keep the information and allow yourself to appreciate the conversation that you just had. Wait a few hours or a few days until you feel that you are ready to contact them again. Sending a quick message to express that you enjoyed talking to them can do a lot for the friendship/relationship. It shows that you care and that you enjoyed their company. The more that you are able to interact before you see one another again, the more you will have to talk about next time.

Make plans to hang out. This is how you keep building on your interaction. Spending time together in person is the best way to truly practice your social skills. Not only are you going to be learning, but you are going to be learning in great company. Feeling that you can facilitate these interactions is great, and it gives you a huge sense of freedom. Now, when you walk into any room or any space, you can feel confident in knowing that you can make friends if you wanted to. Once you are able to set your own worries aside and accept yourself, there is so much that becomes possible.

Talking with Peers

Following some of the same concepts, talking with your peers should be easier than talking to strangers. To start, you already know that you have certain things in common with your peers. Whether you work together or you know each other through a different activity, having peers indicates that you are around other people who are on the same level as you. You might feel like you want to take your friendship to the next level. Instead of only interacting in the workplace about work, you might find that you want to truly get to know a person, for example.

Change up the topics that you discuss. Instead of constantly talking about work, try to involve your other interests. Get a feel for who this person truly is. See if they are willing to open up to you about other things that they enjoy doing. Some people become very reserved and focused in a work setting, so you might need to spend time with them outside of work before you can truly get to know them. There are a few ways that you can go about making this happen.

Try to organize a group meal amongst your peers. By inviting a few people to a place that is not work-related, this gives you all a chance to let loose and be yourselves. There is an understandable desire to be a little bit more censored while in the workplace. This is likely due to the fact that there is a boss or supervisor constantly overseeing you and what you are doing. Being off the clock allows you all to act the way that you want to act and talk about the things that you want to talk about. This is when you will really get to discover your peers' personalities.

During these outings, you will get an idea of who you get along with best. While you might enjoy spending time with the group as a whole, there are likely going to be individual connections that are stronger than the others. Gravitate toward these people and make it a point to get to know them better. Building friendships with the people you work with actually ends up making your work days better. When you have friends at work, you have alliances. These people know exactly how it feels to work at your company and go through the daily struggles that come with the job. It makes sense to get close to them.

Remember, depending on how professional your workplace is, you are going to need to maintain a level of composure while at work. This means that you do not need to be talking loudly and laughing about inside jokes with your friends while you are supposed to be on the clock. While you can be friendly, make sure that you are also being appropriate for the given situation.

Know that you can always hang out in a less formal setting if you'd like to become that expressive and open.

If you are ever having a bad day at work, you can seek out your friends to help guide you through these situations. While you have always worked with these people, forming connections with them will show you that they truly care. You will have people to vent to and vice versa. This can even make your job seem more enjoyable. No one likes the feeling of isolation, so do not put yourself in a situation that allows for it. Know that you always have a choice in the matter.

Forming these friendships with your peers gives you the opportunities to merge your social circles. For example, if you have dinner with your peers, you can invite your spouse along so that they can meet. You can also do the same with your current group of close friends. Merging these circles is great because it allows you to see exactly how much support that you have. When you bring people together with you being a common link, there is a sense of pride that you can take out of the entire situation. If it wasn't for you, perhaps these people would never have met. It all becomes like a domino effect—as you introduce people, they will also meet new people.

Building Connections

As you continue to grow your social circle, you will continue to gain confidence. You will see that the interactions you have are within your control. You get to decide if you'd like to form a friendship or if you'd like the interaction to be fleeing. This is one of the best parts about socialization—there is so much freedom if you are able to recognize it. Through socialization, there are different types of connections that you can build. The following are some of the most common that you will find:

1. Platonic: A platonic relationship is simply a friendship. Those you seek platonic connections with are those you can see yourself being friends with. These are people that you'd like to make it a point to talk to again. You might even desire to spend time in person with this individual. Most connections that you make are going to be platonic in the beginning, even if they eventually evolve. People tend to express platonic energy when they are first interacting with new people.

2. Romantic: A romantic connection happens when you are physically and emotionally attracted to someone in the beginning. You might still desire their friendship, but there is also something about them that causes you to want them on a deeper level. Finding someone you'd like

a romantic connection with is exciting. It does not happen very often, so it is a gift when you come across a person like this. While it can be an experience that causes you to forget all of your great social skills due to your nerves, try your best to take a leap of faith.

3. Acquaintance: This is a person that you might only actively talk to once. It is someone that you do not care to have an active friendship with, yet you do appreciate who they are as an individual. You might meet an acquaintance when you are socializing with people that your current friends know. These are people that you become familiar with, but you do not actively make an effort to spend any time with. Having acquaintances is not a bad thing. In fact, it is the opposite. When you keep acquaintances, you are still growing your social circle. You never know what the future holds. Some people find great friendships or even relationships from those who started out as acquaintances.

4. Professional: Connecting professionally can serve many different purposes. Whether you want friends/acquaintances or to create a business connection that can serve your career, a professional interaction takes a few different skills to build. In general, you need

to put your best self forward. When it comes to seeking out professional connections, you should aim to be polite and more formal than you would be if you were at a party with your friends, for example. Show the other person your best traits, but do so in a way that is controlled. Once the connection develops, you will be able to see how much you can open up.

It is exciting to think about all of the different possibilities that can come from a single interaction. As you build connections with other people, you will grow and develop as a person. The way that others interact with you will solidify your traits and your personality. As long as you can remain true to who you are, no matter who you are talking to, then you can consider yourself an expert conversationalist. You will be able to gain valuable information about yourself while opening your mind to new viewpoints and ideas. This connectivity is the basis of building connections that last.

Chapter 8: Deepening Your Current Friendships

No matter who your friends are, you owe it to them to be a friend who has great things to offer. As you probably have first-hand experience with, being friends with someone who does not value you or does not take the time to check-in with you can feel like you are involved with someone who is selfish. Toxic friendships are dangerous and upsetting, so don't be that type of friend. Know that friendships take work and effort to maintain. You cannot expect to make a bunch of new friends and keep them all by doing nothing in return. You need to be there for them, show them that you care about what is going on in their lives.

If you want to make sure that you are being the greatest friend possible, consider these tips on keeping your friendships active:

- Spend Time Together on a Weekend: When you are able to hang out with someone on a day that is not filled with obligations, you will get the chance to do more of what you want to do. Sunday mornings are normally a great time to spend with people. They are relaxed and open to many possibilities. Ensure that you do not have any other plans that will cut your time short with this person. Have breakfast together, and stay as long as you both want. From here, you can decide what you'd like to do next. Be spontaneous! Consider both your interests so that you can engage in a fun activity that you will both enjoy.

- Become Comfortable with Silence: In friendship, especially those that are well-established, you shouldn't expect every single moment to be filled with conversation. Learn how to accept silence as a treasure. Be comfortable in these moments, and do not feel that you have to fill them just for the sake of filling them. Those who are comfortable with one another, in general, do not need filler conversation in order to maintain this comfort. It might take time to reach this point with your various friendships, but know that accepting silence is not a negative thing. It can provide you with moments of reflection that can be great for the friendship. You might realize how much you enjoy spending this time with one another.

- Reach Out When You Are in Need: Having fun within a friendship is a great feeling, but being able to count on someone when you are unhappy can also be just as great. Make sure that you are working toward confiding in your friends because they are there for you. Whether you need emotional coaching or physical support, you should be able to reach out to your friends when you are in need. This type of reciprocated support system is what will take your friendship to the next level. It can be easy to think of fun things to do, but helping one another in dire times will become even more of a learning experience.

- Make Time for Them: You might have a busy day ahead of you, but when your friend asks you if you can be there for them, you should try your best to be there. Much like romantic relationships, friendships can also come with some forms of sacrifice. You do these things because you care about these people, and the action should be coming from a place of love. Never make your friends feel guilty for the time that you decide to reserve for them. They are just as important and worthy of support as you are. Even if there is not a bad situation unfolding, being there for your friends in general shows that you are committed to the friendship. Anything that you make time for is something you consider important, and it can mean a lot when others see this.

- Share Your Ideas: Your friends can help you develop your ideas. When you are able to brainstorm with them, a creative way of thinking happens. This creativity can take you far by opening your mind to new ideas or inspiring you to seek out new opportunities. It is no secret that friendships can help you grow, and it is a sign of a great friendship when you are able to discuss ideas with one another. Even if your friend isn't doing anything other than listening to you, this might be the exact boost of confidence that you need to keep reaching for your goals.

- Create Together: Working together to create something can be a great way to build your friendship. While you do not need to become business partners, even creating a piece of art together can be a way for you to bond. The creation process is fun and exciting. It becomes even more interesting when you share this with someone that you enjoy spending time with. This process will allow the two of you to come together with your ideas and select the one that you would like to see through. Not only is this fun, but it can help you grow individually.

- Pay Attention to Details: When you first meet someone, you likely aren't going to know every single detail about them. This part comes after some time of getting to know one another. Having attention to detail is a great trait to express within a friendship. From remembering your friends' birthdays to their favorite colors, you will be able to show them how much you care by taking the time to retain these details. Do not consider any detail too large or too small; know that they are all equally important. These details are what make your friends who they are.

- Take a Trip Together: Going on a vacation with your friend is a fun way to bond. While a European vacation might not be realistic for your time and budget, you can still find ways to travel together. Taking a simple road trip together to a nearby town for the day can prove to be just as fun as a whole vacation. When you are exploring a new place together, you will both be at the same starting point. From deciding which route to take and where you'd like to stop for food, you will be coming together with your friend to make these decisions. This is a meaningful way to spend time with one another.

- Share Your Past: Maybe your friends weren't there in your past, but that does not mean that you need to keep this from them. Sharing your past is a way of showing your friends how much you trust them. As you know, your past has a lot to do with the person that you have become today. It provides people with a deeper understanding of why you are the way that you are. If you feel like sharing this with a friend, this is a great thing. It will strengthen your bond and allow for a better understanding of who you are.

These ideas are only meant to get you started with strengthening your friendships. The best ideas come from the heart. You know your friends best, so make sure that you think about different ways to spend time together that will benefit things that you both enjoy doing. The simple idea of trying something new together can be enough to replenish the friendship. Because you are going to be putting in the time and effort to try this new thing, your friend is going to see how committed you are to the friendship.

The best part about friendship is that there are no rules! As long as you are treating one another with kindness and respect, there is nothing that you absolutely *must* do in order to be considered a great friend. What matters most is that you both feel fulfilled within the friendship. If there ever comes a point where you do not feel that you are fully being appreciated, speak up. Your friend won't always realize that you feel this way, so it is better to talk about how you feel and be honest about it instead of holding onto these feelings passive-aggressively. Do not assume that your friend can read your mind. It is within this excellent communication that you will be able to work through anything together.

Know that some people require different types of friendships. Traditionally, a friendship involves speaking to one another often and making the time to see each other in person whenever possible. Some people want what are known as "low maintenance friendships." These are the types of friendships where you do not talk or hang out as often, but you still maintain a successful friendship. Much like your own social abilities, some people are only going to want friendship in small doses. This is okay, as long as both parties are happy and understanding of the dynamic.

Beware of those friendships that drain you. The opposite of low maintenance, having a friend who demands to see you all the time and wants to talk 24/7 can become a bothersome person to have in your life. While it is nice to think that your friend values you so much, it can actually become hindering to you if your friend starts 'punishing' you for the time that you cannot devote to them. This can include giving you the cold shoulder or treating you poorly in general. Be on the lookout for friendships like these because this is an indication of toxicity.

How to Be You

It is easy to become lost in others' habits and mannerisms. While you feel that you might have the hang of socialization and friendship, know that staying true to who you are is still very important. Do not allow the opinions of others to completely take over your own morals and values. You are still your own person, no matter how many friends you acquire along the way. Remember, your true self is what got you these friends, to begin with. If you simply transform into someone else, people might begin to miss the original version of you that you presented them with.

The more time that you spend with someone, the more likely it is that you will pick up on their behaviors. This is something that happens naturally within friendships. Think about the person that you are closest to right now, no matter who it is. Chances are that you have some similarities in the way that you talk, think, and act. This doesn't have to be a bad thing, as long as you remember that you also have your own wonderful traits.

Adopting traits from your friends can be great, as long as you do not completely take on their personality, too.

Spending some time to work on yourself will make you a better friend. Now that you have the ability to make friends and build connections, spending time alone is likely the last thing that you will want. Know that this will benefit all your friendships and future interactions, though. Check-in with yourself regularly and ask yourself if you are being the best version of you that you can. Do you still love the person that you are? If the answer is no, then something must change.

If you stop loving yourself, you might project these insecurities onto your friends. By making them feel unintentionally guilty for not building you up, it can be very easy to become a toxic friend that you would avoid yourself. Know that you can be just as happy alone as you can be with a friend. Hang out with yourself, and get to know yourself as you would another person. While these situations do not have to happen all the time, it is still a good idea to take part in them occasionally so that you know for sure that you still love yourself and the person that you are becoming.

Take the time to reinvent yourself, if you must. Do something new that you are unfamiliar with. When you have more friends, you will likely have more confidence. Know that you can still find ways to challenge yourself that will be different from the ways you utilized before. Put yourself in situations where you do not feel like you know exactly what is going to happen. This is a great way to catch yourself off guard and to really observe how you respond to new situations. You will probably find that there are many more interests that you may find yourself wanting to explore.

When you do not feel like yourself, open up to your friends. They might be able to remind you of the ways that you are truly a great person. It is common to lose sight of ourselves over time. This is something natural that nearly everyone must experience. It can happen a lot in socialization because of the pressure to transform into someone who is liked by the masses. Understand that not everyone has to like you. There is no obligation to please the world. As long as you are happy and you are treating your friends well, feel proud of who you are.

Conclusion

Reaching the end of this guide, you have gone through many essential steps toward becoming great at social interaction. Know that your journey does not end here. Your social skills will always be evolving, so there should never be a point in time where you stop working on them. Continue to thrive, and enjoy showing others the greatest parts of yourself and your personality. Starting from the very beginning, you have learned the definition of "social skills," and how yours have developed throughout your life. By identifying your strengths and weaknesses, you can use these to your advantage.

Moving into specific skill sets, you should now be able to realize the difference between being an active listener and a passive listener. To do so, you need to have a certain level of empathy and understanding for the person you are talking to. This will allow you to become close to people, encouraging you to use your best listening skills. In the same way that you will learn how to be a great listener, you will also learn how to be a great conversationalist. There will be no more moments of getting caught up in your insecurities and doubts. Instead, you will be able to find commonalities that will lead you toward great topics of conversation.

By breaking down the most common fears and worries that you will face when socializing, you will realize that these things do not have to hold you back. By learning to overcome them, you will have the ability to challenge your inner critic and prove to yourself that you are capable. Once you understand that you are going to be disappointed in life at times, you no longer need to let these disappointments prevent you from working toward something better. It becomes a huge help when you are able to differentiate aggressive behavior from assertive behavior. By knowing how to deal with all types of people, you will be better equipped to handle all types of social interaction.

A reminder that manners are an important skill to have will show you that good manners can actually lead you to having more friendships and interactions. The better you present yourself, the better you will be perceived by those around you.

When you can acknowledge the importance of having good manners and treating others with respect, you will be able to make a great first impression on anyone that you encounter. From the way that you speak to the way that you utilize your body language, you will be able to show people the best version of yourself.

Once you get the hang of practicing your social skills, you will be able to apply them toward any new social interactions with the new people you meet. By remembering to rely on your confidence to guide you through social situations, you will feel ready and able to converse with anyone who you want to. Whether you are talking to your peers or complete strangers, you will be able to build meaningful connections that will impact your life for the better. As long as you remain open to the idea of giving other people a chance, you are also being open to the idea that you can continually work on your social skills.

Know that socialization doesn't need to be difficult or scary. While you might still have your insecurities, this does not mean that you aren't ready to talk to other people. The best way to learn is by practicing real applications of the techniques that were discussed. This is how you can become the best version of yourself possible. Don't forget to maintain your current friendships, too. Just because they aren't new anymore doesn't mean that you should take them for granted. All friendships deserve your time and effort. Make sure that you are still making time for those who have been there for you constantly.

As you become more comfortable with opening up to others, you will realize that no one is ever as judgmental as you think they are. We are all human beings with our own insecurities. Most of the time, other people are going to be worrying about their own problems and flaws. They are likely too preoccupied to even pay attention to yours. This is why it is best to just put yourself out there; take a chance and show people the real you from the very beginning. Anyone who does not accept you does not need to become a part of your permanent social circle. Try to surround yourself with those who have loving and caring energy.

Bibliography

Blatt, R. (2013, September 2). 9 Ways to Increase Your Charisma. Retrieved October 10, 2019, from https://www.psychologytoday.com/us/blog/the-rock-band-project/201309/9-ways-increase-your-charisma

Cherry, K. (2019, August 28). Why Is It Important to Use Empathy in Certain Situations? Retrieved October 10, 2019, from https://www.verywellmind.com/what-is-empathy-2795562

G, H. (2019, September 27). Active Listening vs. Passive Listening. Retrieved October 10, 2019, from https://diffzi.com/active-listening-vs-passive-listening/

Kids' Health - Topics -. (2018, August 22). Retrieved October 10, 2019, from http://www.cyh.com/HealthTopics/HealthTopicDetailsKids.aspx?p=335

Manners: Introduction. (2019). Retrieved October 10, 2019, from http://mtstcil.org/skills/manners-intro.html

Mayne, D. (2019, October 2). 10 Benefits of Having Good Manners. Retrieved October 10, 2019, from https://www.thespruce.com/how-you-benefit-from-proper-etiquette-1216688

Michael, J. (2017, May 12). How to Identify Your Strengths and Weaknesses. Retrieved October 10, 2019, from https://articles.bplans.com/how-to-identify-your-strengths-and-weaknesses/

Morin, A. (2015, April 21). Taming Your Inner Critic: 7 Steps To Silencing The Negativity. Retrieved October 10, 2019, from https://www.forbes.com/sites/amymorin/2014/11/06/taming-your-inner-critic-7-steps-to-silencing-the-negativity/

Positive Body Language - Importance - Tutorialspoint. (2019). Retrieved October 10, 2019, from https://www.tutorialspoint.com/positive_body_language/positive_body_language_importance.htm

Shanley, D. (2018, July 8). 7 Ways to Overcome Shyness and Social Anxiety. Retrieved October 10, 2019, from https://psychcentral.com/blog/7-ways-to-overcome-shyness-and-social-anxiety/

Sicinski, A. (2018, December 6). 6 Steps for Overcoming Insecurity and for Regaining Your Self-Confidence. Retrieved October 10, 2019, from https://blog.iqmatrix.com/overcoming-insecurity

Wiest, B. (2015, August 6). 15 Little Ways to Deepen Your Relationship with Anyone. Retrieved October 10, 2019, from https://www.huffpost.com/entry/15-little-ways-to-deepen-your-relationship-with-anyone_b_7949462